The Discipline of Now

12 Practical Principles To Overcome Procrastination

Eric Twiggs

ISBN- 978-0-692-83500-5

Printed in the United States

PROJECT MANAGER: John Peragine • John@JohnPWriter.com

Table of Contents

Foreword

Dr. Willie Jolley here, and I am so glad you have picked up Eric Twiggs's book, *The Discipline of Now*. Procrastination is the biggest "nation" in the world, and it is a big problem.

Procrastination is a challenge that I believe all of us face in our daily lives, but unfortunately, we "put off" doing something about it. The good news is that Eric has cracked the code. He helped develop for you, the reader, ways to overcome procrastination using a unique method.

Not convinced that procrastination is a problem?

I suppose that it is not an issue if you want to put your:
- Dreams
- Achievements
- Results

...On Hold.

Those that don't achieve everything they want in life, fail to do so because they have chosen to hit that "hold" button in their life. The problem is they never take their life off "hold". They die with their dreams still trapped inside of them. You are not one of those people- right?

It may be hard to believe that I, Dr. Willie Jolley, would ever let procrastination get the best of me, but I am guilty. When I wrote my first book it took me five years to complete. Actually, it only took me a few months to complete. It took me five years to get started!

When I first began my speaking career, I not only knew that I needed a book, I had some great ideas for one. It was important. It was a priority. It never got started.

Five years into my career, I became forced by a contractual agreement to write a book. I could not put it off any longer. I completed it, and guess what? It was an instant success and quickly rose the charts to become a best seller.

I had the 20/20 hindsight that Eric talks about in this book to see clearly, I had procrastinated. How many best sellers could I have created in those five years? How could writing the book have pushed my career forward- faster? The answer is I will never know. I could not get those years back, but I had learned a powerful lesson and it now sits as a sign on my desk.

"Do It Now."

I only wish I had this book years ago, but you are fortunate enough to have a guide that will quickly help you erase procrastination from your daily schedule, and fill it with all the things you were meant to achieve.

Dr. Willie Jolley
March, 2017

Introduction
Part One

Hello. My name is Eric and I am a procrastinator.

I admit it. I am not proud of it. Since you are reading this book, you are probably a procrastinator too. Go ahead. Say it out loud. "My name is (fill in the blank), and I am a procrastinator."

Come on don't put it off- just say it.

There you go. That was not so hard. The truth is many, many people are procrastinators, and I blame the universal physics. Matter seeks its lowest state- entropy it's called. Ever been in a comfy chair, with your favorite beverage, and the game on or a good book to read? You sink down into the upholstery. You have reached your lowest state. Any lower and you would be laying on the floor.

It is a comfortable, safe and enjoyable state. We could spend hours there, worried about nothing and feel content. That is until you ran out of your beverage, your team lost, or the book ended badly. At that point, you might look at a clock and wonder where all the time went. You might even feel a pang of terror as you begin to think about all the things you should have been doing. This is the art of procrastination, and we all do it.

We must have moments of rest, and we need to recharge. It is about finding that balance. In this book, you will learn all the different traps of procrastination, but more importantly you will learn how to avoid and deal with them.

When I was in school, from grade school to college, I turned procrastination into an Olympic event. If you Google the term "all-nighter", you might see a picture of me. Sounds like I could do miracles all at the last minute, but I was tanking. My grades took a hit because I was not prepared for tests, and the papers I wrote were rushed and unrefined.

95% of people surveyed report having issues with procrastination. The other 5% have put off responding to the survey!

The reason I refer to myself as a procrastinator, is because I believe improvement is a process and not an event. If I fail to apply the principles, I am just as likely as you to backslide.

Intention vs Execution

Goals begin with an idea, and a concept. We often have great motivation, to begin a project, we have intention. Then something happens, and we become like a squirrel chasing a new nut. We become distracted, and other things begin to fill up our attention. It is only through execution that we can accomplish anything.

The best-laid plans of mice and men often go awry definition. No matter how carefully a project is planned, something may still go wrong with it.
-Robert Burns

We can have the best of intentions and that is just not enough. Procrastination can literally drain all the energy and motivation and attention we have on a project. The reason I have written this book, is to help unify the gap between intention and execution. This book was written for the individual who has the mindset of an entrepreneur. The entrepreneur wants control over their future. Applying the right principles is more important now than ever because you can no longer depend on a company to take care of you.

The principles you will learn originated from my experience conducting over 28,000 coaching and mentoring sessions with business leaders, reading over 100 books on the topic, and my experiences in corporate America where I supervised organizations of 500 or more people. I will also share my personal stories and pain as it relates to procrastination and how I'm using what you are about to learn.

Divide And Conquer

This book is divided into three sections:

Costs of Procrastination

The Causes

The Cure

It is important to know the nature of procrastination and how it can creep into our lives without even a hello. I have sat down with the intention to complete this book, and then I find I am working on the same paragraph two days later. How does that happen? Procrastination is a tricky and sly beast, but one which can be slain with execution.

Do not skip the first two sections with the thought you understand procrastination. I structured this book in such a way that it is interactive. You must complete one section and do as I instruct immediately before proceeding to the next.

Get ready. Roll up your sleeves. You have work to do, so do not delay- get to chapter one already!

1

The Costs of Procrastination

I was recently watching an old game on the NFL network between the Washington Redskins and the New Orleans Saints. The Redskins were beating the Saints badly, that is until the 4th quarter. The saints changed their strategy to a two-minute offense. For those that don't know what that is, it is also called the hurry up offense. The goal is to move quicker in order to score as many points as possible before time runs out. The team gets to the line quicker, and they don't even huddle. They are moving fast with more hustle.

The outcome was that the Saints scored more points in the last quarter than they had in the other three quarters combined. The cost was they still lost the game. Their strategy was good, it was just too late. If they had taken this approach the entire game, they had a good chance of winning. They had procrastinated and it cost them.

What Is Procrastination Costing You?

Were you one of those kids in school that knew about a project weeks in advance, and then the night before the project was due, you began working on it? What did this level of procrastination cost you? A letter grade? Two letter grades? The fact is that if you are studying for a test and trying to memorize facts, you are relying on just your short-term memory. This is not a good way to remember facts and figures. Here is a simple test to prove it.

Here are 7 digits. Look at them for 10 seconds, and then close the book and write them down. No cheating.

3788956

How did you do? Now can you recall your phone number? How about the phone number of someone close to you? How about the phone number your parents had when you were growing up?

Amazing, right? Just seven digits, yet you have instant recall. Why? It is because through repetition and only allowing your mind to process those phone numbers, the number became imbedded in your long-term memory. When you cram overnight, the information does not have time to be encoded in your long-term memory.

In his book, *Make It Stick*, Peter C. Brown points out that cramming for a midterm test doesn't lead to mastery of the material because the information is stored in short term memory. He concludes that study that is spread out over time produces better test results because the information is stored in long term memory which leads to mastery and longer retention.

Maybe this habit of procrastination followed you into college or even into the workplace. Do you still wait until the last minute to complete a project?

Many people tell me that they work better under pressure. That is a justification for procrastination. They say they perform better under dire conditions, but there are several reasons that I do not believe this to be true, that I will explore with you in this chapter.

Procrastination is a habit, which is the good news and the bad news. It is bad news in that you are more likely to repeat the behavior even though the consequences are high. It is the same issue for those who speed while driving. Even when a person gets a ticket, if they are in the habit of driving fast, they are more likely to speed again in the future, which is why their insurance premiums are high. Insurance companies consider people who are caught speeding a high risk, and statistically they will continue the potentially deadly habit.

The good news is that because it is habit, it can be broken and replaced with more beneficial habits. It takes time and practice. This book will teach you how and give you the necessary tools to squash procrastination.

The alternative is that you will continue to pay the costs of procrastination. Below I have listed some of these costs. Some you may have thought about, some you may not have. There are even more than are listed here. You must decide whether procrastination is really the best strategy for achieving the outcomes you are after.

Costs Of Procrastination

Poor quality is a risk. I have already mentioned that in school procrastination can result in lower grades. The risk in business is reduced quality in what you do. There is a link between innovation and preparation. The more prepared you are, the more creative and focused you can be. If you are running against the clock, guess what? You will be watching the clock. Your anxiety will get in your way and shift your focus to finishing, rather than quality and creativeness. I have designed the following "Creativity Matrix" to illustrate the point.

Deadline Urgency High/ Creativity Low	Deadline Urgency High/ Creativity High
Deadline Urgency Low/ Creativity High	Deadline Urgency Low/ Creativity Low

The Four Quadrants

Quadrant #1 Deadline Urgency High/ Creativity Low

You have waited until the last minute. The stress of the looming deadline limits creativity. The brain produces the stress hormone cortisol which has a negative effect on memory and creativity.

Quadrant #2 Deadline Urgency Low/Creativity High

This is the ideal quadrant to operate in. Ideas have time to incubate and you have time for trial and error.

Quadrant #3 Deadline Urgency High/Creativity High

Life circumstances have forced you to be creative. You write a daily column, a daily blog, you get called on at the spur of the moment to give a toast at a wedding. The key to succeeding in this quadrant is to have repeatedly practiced the skill in the past so that when called on you are ready. In this quadrant you don't get ready, you stay ready. An example of this would be a church pastor who receives a call to deliver a sermon at another church with only 24 hours' notice. This pending sermon has a high deadline urgency, but his creativity in this situation would be high thanks to his years of experience and practice delivering sermons.

Quadrant #4 Deadline Urgency Low/ Creativity Low

This quadrant usually represents activities that you have said yes to that don't align with your purpose, passions, and priorities. In the coming chapters, we will discuss how to say no to these types of activities.

You sacrifice a lot by waiting until the last minute. Do you want people to know you for the quality of the work you produce? Then you better get with the program and get started right now.

Health Risks

Procrastination is hard on your health. When we wait until the last minute this leads to stress. Our bodies are wired to respond to stress in a very specific and physical way. Often referred to as the fight or flight response, when we experience stress our body prepares to fight to the death or to run for the hills. It does this by releasing cortisol and other hormones into our body. This gets our heart pumping, more oxygen to the muscles and it increases our strength. We are prepared to punch or leap.

There are some inherent problems with this response. This system called the Sympathetic Nervous System, allowed us to run from predators or to protect ourselves in a fight, or to become a better hunter. We don't encounter many saber-toothed tigers anymore, but the system still exists in our body. The problem is that our body does not differentiate different stressors. Waiting until the last minute to type a report activates the same internal system as running from a gator.

These hormones can wreak havoc on our body. Stress has been linked to heart disease, kidney disease and even certain forms of Cancer. In addition, it lowers our immune system and makes us more likely to get sick.

It is a well-known fact on university campuses that there is always a rise in colds and other infections around midterm and during finals. This is because of the stress levels going up and immunity going down.

We cannot remove stress from our lives, but we can reduce it. By not procrastinating we feel more in control, more confident and less stressed. Stress reduces performance, because we are not loose and ready.

Unfinished tasks produce stressful feelings because we were created with a natural desire to complete what we start. Brian Tracy, business author and speaker, refers to this as a compulsion to closure. Therefore, checking off a completed item on your to-do list creates a feeling of satisfaction, and provides the motivation to begin the next task. An incomplete task creates stress because it conflicts with your innate desire for closure.

Risk Making Less Money

How much money are you leaving on the table? You know companies are counting on your laziness and are profiting from it. How many times have you bought something because there was a nice rebate that came with it? Two things usually happen. One is you just never get around to sending in the material to get the rebate. We like instant rebates because they don't take much thought or energy. When we are forced to mail it in with all the proper documentation, it quickly slides to the bottom of the priority list. The second thing companies count on is that you will miss the deadline. Often rebates have a certain postmarked date or they are not valid. How much money have you thrown away doing that?

Rental fees are another way companies make their real money. You get a video from one of those machines for $1.99, and in the end, you pay triple or even more, because you did not return it on time. That is just free money to the rental company. Do you have money to burn?

Credit card companies and even utility companies tack on late fees for payment. Paying is so easy these days. You can push a button on a smartphone and get it done, yet in an average year, what are you paying in late fees? Do you enjoy giving your hard-earned money away?

Do you realize that the IRS collects over $500 million dollars a year in additional taxes due to late filing? There is no mystery to the date of April 15th. It is the same date every year, so how does the IRS make so much extra money?

You are either a very, very generous person that hates the idea of a savings account, or your procrastination habits are doing harm to your wallet.

Damaged Brand

You probably know that one person that is late to everything. You can expect them not to arrive in the morning on time, and they are consistently late to meetings. Do you know anyone that would promote the person who is consistently late to everything? Are you that person?

During my career in corporate America, I—never overheard the following statement being made by senior level executives: "Let's promote that guy in the accounting department who is always late!" What is your image and brand worth to you? There is a lot of talk about differentiation in the marketplace. Procrastination is a great way to be noticed and labelled, but is that the label you are after?

When you try to sneak into the door or into a meeting, you are not fooling anyone. People notice. You are chipping away at your brand every time it happens.

Bad Luck Magnet

In college, I can recall waiting until the night before a paper was due for a class. It counted for a big percentage of my grade. While I was working on it, my computer crashed. It was bad luck.

I went to my professor the next day and explained the situation to ask for an extension. As you might guess, I got no sympathy from him, and my grade tanked as a result. I should have made at least a "B" in the class, but I ended with a "C".

The truth is, procrastination was the cause of my bad luck. If I had not waited so long, I would not have been in the position I had created for myself. If my computer crashed early in the process, then I would have had plenty of time to fix it and recover.

Have you ever noticed that when you are in a rush, things seem to go wrong? Part of it is that you are more prone to errors and mistakes when you are under the pressure of the clock.

Before I ever do a speaking engagement, I arrive at least an hour early. I want to own the stage and be sure everything is prepared. Many times, when I arrive the seating is wrong, there are technical issues with the microphone and sometimes the emcee does not have my introduction. If I arrive only minutes before an engagement, I might feel I was a victim or that I just had a string of bad luck.

Fortune favors the prepared mind.
-Louis Pasteur

You Might Be A Procrastinator If...

1.You say a prayer under your breath to just get you through this one day and next time you won't wait until the last minute, and you repeat that prayer daily.

2. You believe due dates are merely suggestions.

3. You love the concept of being "fashionably late"

4. You believe time moves differently for you and it has a grudge against you.

5. You believe that if you did not have bad luck, you would have no luck at all.

Persistence Is What Creates Luck

There is the "Law of large numbers" which was supported by Jacob Bernoulli a 1700's mathematician. He stated that many repeated actions over time produces the desired results. If you work hard and continue working hard every day, you will eventually get the results you are after. Instead of waiting for your lucky break, you must become diligent and persistent.

There is an exception to the Law of Large Numbers- the lottery. It does not matter how many times you play; the odds are never in your favor.

Tired of Speeding Tickets?

There is a saying- to be on time is to be early, which means you start earlier and plan. Being late, is not an excuse. You must take 100% responsibility for your actions. Are you tired of paying the tickets and having outrageous insurance rates? People often speed because they left too late. They do not leave any room for traffic or other hazards and so again they may feel they are a victim of bad luck, when they are actually a victim of procrastination and poor planning. I have over ten years' experience when it comes to supervising employees. During that time, I have never had an employee say the following: "Sorry I'm late, I need to leave my house earlier." What I would hear is, "Traffic was really bad today!"

Damage to Relationships

Relationships, at least the ones that last, are built on trust. If you always wait until the last minute to do things when they are critical, other people will have a difficult time trusting and relying on you. This can damage not only work relationships, but personal ones as well.

Consider the following questions:

- Do you wait until the last minute to buy a gift only to find there is nothing to select from?
- Are you chronically late to dates?
- Were you late to your own wedding?
- Do people say that you will be late to your own funeral?
- Do you find yourself always rushing around and forgetting things?

If so, you might be a procrastinator.

Short Term And Long Term Gains

With the potential for loss on many levels, why do we do it? Why do we procrastinate? There must be some sort of gains, as we rarely do anything for no reason at all. In most cases, it is for the short-term gain.

People feel better in the short term to avoid pain. There is an immediate gratification. It is a release of anxiety. If you surf the Internet instead of concentrating on a work assignment, you can find the temporary and immediate release from anxiety.

Suppose you are on a diet. You are hungry and there is a slice of your favorite kind of pie, with a scoop of your favorite ice cream on top. I'm making you hungry aren't I?

Do you walk by the pie or eat it? If you are looking for the short-term gain, you just eat the pie.

If you pass it up and look for a celery stalk (I know, I know, just stick with me. No one passes the pie), you are thinking about your long-term gain. Defeating procrastination is passing up the short-term gain, and keeping your eye on the prize of the long-term benefit.

If you work on a project slowly and methodically over time, your outcome will always be greater than a two-minute offense.

What is your priority?

STOP- READ- ACT

In this section of the chapter I will challenge you to close the book and make a definitive step toward your life goals. They can be small steps, but the caveat is that you must do them right NOW! Not tomorrow, not next week. Do not move on to the next chapter until you have completed your task. If you cannot do these small challenges, how equipped are you to overcome your procrastination?

The immediate challenge is take a piece of paper and fold it vertically. One on side write down one thing you procrastinate at, and on the other write down what it is costing you. Do no more than 10 of these. Look carefully at that list every day and try to change each one of them. You have total control over whether you procrastinate or not.

What are you still reading for? Close the book and do your task- NOW!

2
Lack Of Clarity

I remember being a senior at Hampton University. I had my whole life ahead of me, but I was just thinking about when the next frat party started.

I asked my close friend Donnell one day, "What are your plans after graduation?"

"Well that's easy. I have always dreamed of becoming a Marine Corps officer. How about you?"

"I don't know," I responded. "But, I do know that I am going to a frat party Friday night."

"Seriously though Eric. You must stop wasting time and figure it out."

"I know, I know. But we are still young. We have plenty of time to figure it all out. So, does that mean you are not going to the party with me?"

We both laughed at that a bit. Several weeks later I received news that was anything but funny. My good friend Donnell was killed in a car accident.

Maybe we don't have all the time we think we do.

Donnell and I were a lot alike. We were both from the DC area. We were line brothers in our fraternity. He had purpose in life. My purpose was to party. I thought college was all about having a good time, then you graduated and got a high paying job.

I could not figure out why Donnell always got up at 5:00 AM to jump out of a perfectly good plane. He trained hard for the military, and I just did not understand.

After his death, I decided that I wanted to make as much money as I could in the shortest time possible. I did not care what it took, or what kind of job I had. His passing gave me a new sense of urgency. I was determined to climb the corporate ladder.

Seven years later I had done just that. I was at the top, and I was driving around in my silver BMW. I was the district manager in a national automotive chain, and I had 500 employees that reported to me. We had won the award for having the most profitable district in the entire organization.

I thought I was all that with whipped cream and a cherry on top. I was big. I was bad. I was broken.

One morning as I started up my silver BMW, I looked in the rear-view mirror. The person looking back dreaded going to work.

How could this be?

I made more than my father ever did, and I had the car to prove it. I shared my feelings with my father. I respected him a lot and needed guidance.

"Dad, I hate my job and I am about to turn in my letter of resignation," I began.

"Son, I understand your feelings. But, what is your next move?"

"I'm not sure, but maybe quitting will buy me the time to figure it out."

"Son, I love you to death, but moving back home is off the table." He was serious. "So, before you decide to quit, I want you to answer a couple questions. What are you passionate about? When do you feel driven?"

As I reflected on my father's questions, I thought about the quote by Michael Josephson- 'It's not what you drive. It's what drives you.'

Short Cuts

I was not ready to give up my lifestyle, I just figured I needed to find another high paying job in a different industry. I had years of experience and an education. It should be a piece of cake to move laterally into another position.

At the time, I knew several people who were making good salaries as pharmaceutical reps. I went to a recruiter and I was ready for a new adventure.

"I want to be a pharmaceutical rep. Here is my resume."

The recruiter looked it over and then looked up at me, "Are you serious? Why would anyone hire you as a pharmaceutical rep? Do you have any experience doing that?"

"No but, look at all the things I did as a district manager and look at my education," I countered.

"None of that makes you qualified to shift into another industry. I am sorry. I could help you with work within the automotive industry," he offered.

I did not want to find another job just like the one I had. I had a good job with a good company. I just did not like the work I was doing. I wanted out even though I was making good money. There was something missing in my plan- a clear vision.

Three Years

Some people are slow learners when it comes to procrastination. I was unhappy, but I was putting off how to really fix it. I thought about my father's questions to me again.

What are you passionate about?

When do you feel driven?

I took the time to reflect on these questions. I thought about all the jobs I had in my life and which ones that I enjoyed doing. A pattern very quickly emerged- I enjoyed speaking and coaching. This was the area I wanted to work in.

Why wasn't I doing something about it? Why was I putting it off?

I finally understood Donnell's desire to wake up 5:00 AM every day. His dream to become a Marine was driving him.

Once I gained that level of clarity about my life, it set off a very interesting chain of events. First my company called me and offered me a training position that would allow me to speak to audiences of executives. Shortly thereafter, I was offered a position as a business coach with another organization.

I had the realization that once you become clear on your vision, you will attract your passions. I thought that I was waiting on the right opportunity but it turns out that the right opportunities were waiting on me.

Once I became clear, then I began taking steps toward my goal. I want to be clear about something. To achieve your goals and dreams, it takes hard work and time to achieve them. The overnight success stories usually were a decade's worth of work. When we finally succeed at our intended goals, it might seem that opportunities occur overnight. What is really happening is that we worked until the opportunity came to us.

The time it takes to achieve something is not the same as procrastination. Just because we cannot make things happen instantly in our lives does not mean we are being lazy. When you put a cake in the oven, it just takes time for the cake to bake. Turning up the heat only results in a burnt half cooked cake. Procrastination, is like thinking about baking that cake but never cracking an egg.

Creating Your Own Vision

Once I had my vision, then I could begin taking the appropriate steps to making it a reality. I began with becoming a member of Toastmasters International. It was here that I would begin to sharpen my skills. This took some time, but at least I was in a forward momentum. Each subsequent step became clear- a webpage, developing leads, honing my keynote speech, blogging, and more. I was motivated to accomplish each because I was passionate about what I was doing. This helped to short circuit the procrastination robot in my brain.

In a 2012 Gallup Survey they found that 87% of the workforce is disengaged (24% actively disengaged, 63% not engaged, 13 %

emotionally invested.) I was a part of the 87% that was disengaged. Where do you fall?

I believe many people are disengaged because of the lack of clarity in their life. It is important that you too achieve and define your passion with clarity. Below are a couple of ways you can begin to achieve this.

Letter From The Future

To gain clarity of where you want to go, you can write a letter from yourself twenty years in the future, in which you describe what life is like. It forces you to be your future self and in the process, you gain that clarity I am speaking of.

Dear Eric,

This is from your future self. I am so happy with the way my life turned out. I am a bestselling author of three books, and I am travelling the world talking to audiences and spreading my message…

STOP- READ- ACT

Pull out a piece of paper and write the letter. I do not give you permission to go to the next exercise until you have completed it. It will not take you long to complete. I can almost hear all the voices in your head giving you excuses, as to why you cannot do this right now. Look the next page is blank- write it there. Just find a pen, a crayon, an eye liner. Get writing.

Deathbed Self

Another way to push your mind toward clarity is to imagine you are in your deathbed. I know it sounds morbid, but stick with me.

What would your deathbed self say that you needed to get accomplished in the time you had remaining? You want to write a book? You better get on it. You want to jump from a plane? You better schedule a time.

You want to be a dancer? You want to be nurse? Whatever it is, imagine your deathbed self is telling you to start the process now, because tomorrow may be too late.

STOP- READ- ACT

Write on the next page what your deathbed self would tell you that you must get done today. Don't try to be tricky here- you still have that pen you found in the "packet drawer" in your kitchen. Get writing!

Vision Statement

You should have some great notes related to your vision. I want you to condense them into one or two sentences, on the next page. It should be clear and actionable. Here is my vision statement: *My vision is to become the world's leading authority on the topic of overcoming procrastination.*

STOP- READ- ACT

Yes, I am going to direct you again. WRITE YOUR VISION STATEMENT. Put the phone down. The apocalypse is not going to be announced on Facebook, so you can wait to look. Get this done. Here are three questions to ask yourself to help clarify your vision:

1. What am I passionate about?

2. What does success mean to me?

3. If I could make a difference for anyone or any cause, what would that difference be?

Mission Statement

You should have your vision statement now. Right?

The next step is to begin to create a plan to achieve your vision. My vision was to be a professional speaker. My mission statement was to be more tactile- I needed to learn the business of professional speaking. I needed to hone my craft. So, I joined Toastmasters International. Below is my Mission Statement.

My mission is to serve God, to provide for and protect my family, and to inspire people through communication to find and follow their calling in life.

Core Values

There was a basketball coach who coached in the Midwest for 15 years experiencing moderate success. Everything changed when he established specific core values for him and his teams to follow. The coach was John Wooden of the UCLA Bruins and his teams went on to win 10 national championships in a 12-year time span.

Companies establish core values to help them clarify what they do and why they do what they do. Leaders of organizations with established core values are less likely to procrastinate on making key decisions. As with an organization, people who have personal core values make better decisions and have an easier time moving forward. These values help to establish and determine your priorities. Reviewing the questions from the personal mission exercise will help you to establish your core values

My Core Values:

Family - Since family is a high priority, time I waste at the office being unproductive is time I am taking away from my family. If I don't get things done, I must take work home. Since I value family, I am motivated to be fully present when I am with them.

Excellence - The earlier I start on a creative project, the greater chance it has of being excellent. As mentioned earlier, there is a link between innovation and preparation. Valuing excellence motivates me to start earlier.

Integrity - This motivates me to finish what I start and to do what I say I will do. I make certain goals public knowing that I will be motivated to stay true to my word.

Many years have passed since my life changed and I have not dreaded a single morning. I understand the passion and vision that Donnell had, and now I have incorporated both in my life. Today I drive an awesome silver Toyota Camry.

How Do You Know It's Working?

When people who don't know about your established core values, are always complimenting you based on how you demonstrate them. For example, if people from different walks of life, compliment me for having a high standard of excellence, it confirms that I am on the right track.

3
Fear

Success happens on the other side of your fears- Eric Twiggs

Congratulations, you made it to chapter 3. Why is this a big deal? Studies show that most people begin reading a book and don't make it past chapter 2. How long did it take to you to get this far? A couple hours? A day? Are there flying cars now, and we get our food for the day in a pill?

I never like to assume things about people, so you may feel that I overstate things. I want to be sure you are crystal clear on your vision, and can execute your life in ways you never imagined.

Disclaimer

These usually go in the beginning of the book, but I did not want to scare you off. I figure by chapter 3, we have a good enough relationship, which allows me to share with you the absolute truth about this book.

This book is NOT for everyone. If you like the trajectory of your life, just pass this on to someone else.

There is no secret pill here. I am not offering a shortcut or any ridiculous promises, except one. If you work harder than you ever have in your life, and beat down procrastination like one of those gophers' heads in one of those arcade games with a hammer, you WILL experience results.

Many people have read the book titled: "The Secret." They believe if they wished hard enough, create vision boards, and hang them prominently in their office that this is going to be their year. Here is the harsh reality: If you fail to act, these collages are just pictures of things you won't have.

There is no shortcut to happiness. There is no shortcut to greatness. There is only a clear vision, and hard, tactile work to get to the top of the mountain that lays before you.

If you want an empty promise of a shortcut, bring this book back to bookstore and ask for a refund. If you are ready to stop making excuses and get off your duff and do something, then keep reading. We are only getting started.

Fear

Fear is intimately connected with procrastination. If we fear something, we naturally tend to avoid it. Sometimes this is in a direct fashion- if you don't like snakes, you don't go into the snake house at the zoo. Often though, we put things off we are afraid of. For instance, if you want a raise, you may think of a 1001 other things to do rather than talk to your boss about it.

This is connected to a flight or fight response. When we fight, we confront our fears and deal with the situation. It does not mean we are not afraid of it, it means we dig deep to find the willpower to overcome our fear. In fact, when we do this, and succeed at overcoming our fear, it often disappears from our lives. If you are afraid of snakes, but overcome that fear to hold one, your fight or flight response is short circuited. You no longer have anything to fear.

Our flight response is to get away from the thing we are afraid of. We can literally run away. We see a snake in our backyard and we run screaming like a 4-year-old girl. Often, our flight is much subtler, and this is when procrastination occurs. We put off facing our fear, and find other things to do in our avoidance.

This can happen in romantic relationships. We think we are into another person, and then we find out we are not as into them as much as they are into us. So instead of facing the fear of a nasty breakup, we put it off, and put it off and put it off, and in some unlucky situations we become a run-away bride or groom.

At work, we avoid conflict because we are afraid. We allow a situation to build until it becomes ugly and toxic. Sometimes it is the fear of leaving a company that can freeze us into a position we hate.

I have broken fear into four main categories in relation to procrastination. These four areas often generate situations that we avoid confronting and overcoming. First you must recognize that fear exists and in what form. Then you can eradicate it with the right action steps.

Fear Of Failure

When I was in college, I used to play this little game with myself- it was the false win/win game of lowering the bar. I had this fear that maybe I wasn't smart enough. When it was test time, I always prepared for the worst. I expected it.

If I did well on a test, it was a win. I would then say to myself, "Wow, if I had studied even more, maybe I could have gotten a higher grade."

If I failed I would say, "The reason I failed is because I waited until the last minute to study. I just ran out of time." Since either outcome was a win, I never tested my limits.

This occurred because I was afraid of failing. I set myself up to fail by procrastinating and creating my future reality. I avoided giving it my all, because I didn't know if my all was good enough.

The truth is that failing is a better indicator of success than not trying. The Belgian physical chemist, Ilya Prigogine conducted a Nobel Prize winning Bike Riding Study. In it he showed that falling off a bike and failing when we first learn to ride is a good thing, because it begins to shape our brains. It embeds the experience and provides us with better ways to succeed. When we finally do succeed, all the information is forever stamped on our brains. Therefore, if you have not ridden a bike in many years, you can quickly remember how to do it. You don't have to learn the process all over again.

Giving into the fear of failure not only sets you up to fail, it prevents your brain from learning how to succeed. Why are you blocking yourself?

In her book Mindset, author Carol Dweck talks about two different kinds of mindsets- fixed and growth. The fixed mindset is the belief that we have what we have in life and that we have no way to change it. It is the limiting belief that we are stuck and unable to do anything more in life than we have achieved. For example, intelligence- we have a certain IQ and so we cannot become any smarter. This is at the foundation of the fear of failure. "Why should I try to become a doctor? I am just not smart enough. I am not good enough in math. I am not good enough in science. I don't want the embarrassment of trying to be something I am not."

The growth mindset is the one that successful people have. It is the belief we can grow and learn and that we need to try and fail to learn how to succeed. This is in alignment with the Bike Riding Study. If you're not good in math, then get better. Get a tutor. Study harder. Study longer. You may not be a rocket scientist, but you can improve your math skills. If you allow the fear of failure to dictate your actions, you have committed to failure.

Fear Of Success

We receive so many mixed messages about success. On the one hand, we are supposed to be driven to succeed, but on the other hand, too much success can be a bad thing. We carry the belief that wealthy people are bad people. They are people that get tax breaks and suppress the underclasses whenever they can.

Then, there is the herd mentality. This is more deeply rooted in our DNA. Our ancestors stayed close to one another and formed tribes. This was for safety and survival. Those who stood out from the crowd, were less likely to survive, as they would be food for a saber tooth tiger. No one wanted to be put out of the tribe as it could be a death sentence.

Today, we still tend to cling closely to the herd. If we progress vertically toward success, we are moving out of the herd. We have an innate feeling of being alone and banished from our peers. Have you ever experienced getting a promotion and suddenly all your peers at work hated you for it? Is the sacrifice of success worth the cost? If you want to really succeed it is.

Within this herd mentality is a pull toward mediocrity. If we speak up in a meeting and present a new idea, we may end up saddled with heading a committee around the idea. We have just created more work for ourselves. We remain silent because it is safer and we seem to get along better. If you want to stay exactly where you are, then do nothing. It works. Mediocrity is safe and ensures our voice is never heard and that we will be lost in the crowd.

Fear Of The Unknown

Here is a story you may have heard before, but it clearly illustrates why we often procrastinate when it comes to change.

Kim moved into a new neighborhood and she noticed that the dog next door was howling a lot. She thought it was just a passing thing and that eventually the dog would stop.

"Howlllll…. Howlllll" The dog never relented. After a day. After two days. After a week, the dog was still howling and so Kim decided to make a visit to her neighbor Mr. Simon. When she approached the porch, there was the dog, howling and wailing. Mr. Simon was sitting with the morning paper, sipping his coffee and not seeming to react to his howling dog.

"Mr. Simon," said Kim, "I have noticed that your dog is howling day and night. Is there something wrong with her?"

Mr. Simon slowly sipped his coffee and replied, "Yes, she is howling because she is sitting on a nail."

Kim was taken aback by this reply, "But why does she just howl? Why doesn't she move?"

Without missing a beat Mr. Simon replied, "Because the nail does not hurt enough yet."

We fear what we cannot see. That is why we are afraid of the dark, because our minds can insert all sorts of dangers hiding and waiting for the chance to pounce. Again, this is deep in our DNA, and this sort of fear in many situations can be helpful. It is not helpful when it comes to personal growth and development. We often put off what we should be doing because we are afraid of imagined consequences. This is sometimes referred to as disaster fantasies. We imagine the worst scenarios and unfortunately, we avoid them, even if they are not real.

Trying something new can be scary. Even writing this book forced me to confront fears of failing or not knowing what I was doing. Obviously, if you are reading this, I worked through my fear. Many people, however, do not.

The greatest way to grow in your career is to really hate your job. What I mean by that is if you hate your job you are more likely to look for a better position. If you just mildly dislike your job, you will stay there forever. Sticking to a job that is only a little annoying may seem to some to be a good thing.

You would be like the dog lying on the nail, in that the pain of staying put hasn't outweighed the pain of making the change.

If you were content with your life and your position, I doubt you would have read this far. I believe the nail is hurting. It is time to move.

Overcoming fear is about taking a risk. There are smart risks and foolish ones. Sometimes they are hard to separate, and it is fear that causes the indecision.

A few decades ago people stayed with companies in positions because they had some job security. In addition, they had what is now a mythical creature, a pension. They would retire after a certain number of years, and they and their spouse would be able to live comfortably off a pension that the company provided until death.

We, and I mean all of us, no longer have that type of security. If you are not looking for a plan B or even a plan C, you could wake up tomorrow to a "laid off" notice that you never saw coming. Staying in one position has become riskier than looking to new horizons. If you want to procrastinate and wait for the writing on the wall to become a reality, you could find your future at risk.

We don't know whether risks are legitimate or foolish disaster fantasies. You must have faith in your vision, and you must move forward toward that vision. Take the necessary risks, and be confident that at times you will fail. Each time this happens you will learn, and grow and succeed the next time.

Fear Is In The Future

In 1967, two researchers named Walter Fenz and Seymour Epstein did a study of 22 skydivers that monitored their heart rates. Before they jumped, their heart rates were elevated, but once they leapt from the plane, their rates dropped. It was the fear of what could happen that made them nervous rather than the reality of what happened. Now I am not advocating jumping from a perfectly good plane to prove a point, but we spend a lot of time in the world of "what if".

- What if I fail?
- What if I succeed?
- What if I lose money?
- What if I must move?
- What if she says yes to a date?

This is an indication of the fear of the future. This is different than the fear of the unknown, because we have more control. When the backyard is dark, and we cannot see, we cannot control what might be lurking there. We must either take a risk or stay inside.

The future is what we create. We often act as though we have no control of what happens next, but we absolutely do. Disaster fantasies of what can happen keep us frozen in place because of the power we give them.

I am not advocating foolish risks, instead I am saying you can reduce risk. If you are afraid to branch off and start your own business you might have the following fears:

- If I fail, I may go bankrupt.
- If I fail, I may not get my position back.
- If I succeed, I will have no time for my family.
- If I succeed, I will become overwhelmed and not be able to fulfill orders.

The list can be extensive, but there is one thing that each of these are missing- preparation. You can make preparations to mitigate risk.

If I fail, I may go bankrupt.

Preparation- Start a savings account before you begin and create a buffer.

If I fail, I may not get my position back.

Preparation- Don't leave your position. Ease into the new career before taking the leap.

If I succeed, I will have no time for my family.

Preparation- Be sure you manage your time well. Put family time on your calendar and hold it as sacred as a meeting with a client.

If I succeed, I will become overwhelmed and not be able to fulfill orders.

Preparation- Do not over promise. Start slowly and have a plan of growth you can handle that includes hiring people, and building your capital.

STOP- READ- ACT

I want to you make a quick list of preparations you need to make to take the next step in your growth. List at least three. Pick the top one and do it right now. Put down the book and read no further and just begin the preparation. Each day pick another item on your list and do it. No excuses. No procrastination. Just do it.

4

Perfectionism

You can either be judged because you created something or ignored because you left your greatness inside of you.
-James Clear

Perfectionism Is The Enemy Of Progress

As I had mentioned, it took me at least three years from the time I had the idea and inspiration to become a professional speaker to becoming one. 20/20 hindsight is a wonderful thing because we can have clarity of what is behind us and trace our steps to where we are today. Our futures can sometimes be more unsure and hazy, but at least we are in control of the outcomes. What we did or did not do yesterday, we cannot change, but there is so much we can learn.

I realize now that one of the things that added to my procrastination was a sense of perfectionism. I wanted to control and perfect every aspect of a career as a professional speaker. I did not want to take risks. I wanted to have a clear vision of absolute success with no risk of failure. What I have learned is that perfectionism is the enemy of progress.

I begin a litany of self-doubt within myself.

Why would anyone pay ME to speak?

Wasn't everything I thought about speaking about already said?

I already had a demanding day job, how would I find time to build a perfect, sustainable, speaking business?

The Lizard Brain

Our amygdala is that primal, lizard part of our brain that is scanning for danger. Again, it does not know the difference between a saber-toothed tiger and a third-grade teacher, it just responds danger. It causes us to doubt in order to be safe.

"Don't walk across that field," the lizard brain says, "You are ill prepared. You may get trampled. You are not quick enough to run. You don't have a weapon to protect yourself. You are not smart enough to out maneuver a giant tiger. Stay in the coconut tree where it is safe."

This is useful, although eventually you would have to slide down that tree or starve, but honestly you could be up there awhile.

Let's translate to modern dangers.

"You better not step out of that job. You have no idea what you are getting into. You could end up crushed by debt and have no work and lose everything. You are better off staying in that job where it is safe. You are not prepared. You don't have the right schooling. You are not a business person. You are not..."

There you are, stuck up in a coconut tree where it is safe. You could be there a very long time trying to figure out how to perfectly make a transition into a new job or position. You could be up that tree for a very long time.

Where Do These Messages Come From?

"Eric, do motivational speakers ever have a bad day? With everything that happens in life, how can you be positive ALL the time?" These questions were posed to me at a recent speaking engagement and they got me thinking.

Even those of us that are paid for our positivity have negative experiences. I am no different from you. What separates me from a pessimist is my belief that your perspective determines your progress.

How you perceive what happens to you is more important than the actual event itself. A person with a negative outlook is more likely to procrastinate because he views his setbacks as a stumbling block instead of a stepping stone.

Where were these messages of perfectionism coming from? Why was I paralyzed and unable to move forward? Was there something else at play?

Humans are a collection of habits, which are often grown from beliefs. From habits grow our actions. When you were little, you were probably told that you needed to brush your teeth every day or your teeth would rot out. Your belief created a daily habit. Your daily habit created a routine of getting up and brushing your teeth every morning, after every meal, and at night before bed. What do you mean you are not brushing your teeth four times a day? Shame on you.

We are brought up believing certain things, and these beliefs create certain ways we act and think. When I was in grade school, handwriting was still a thing. You were given this newspaper grade paper with lines on them. Two solid lines, and a dotted line between them. I learned to draw letters and then words in cursive. I wrote the same letter over and over until the teacher said I had mastered it. I had to work until it was perfect or I got a bad grade. A bad grade meant angry parents because they too felt that handwriting was important. So, this instilled in me the idea of perfection. There were a lot of things that supported that idea that I needed it to be perfect or it just was not good enough.

This became a belief, which created a habit of thinking that I needed to have perfect execution or not execute at all. I had to master my letters before I dared write cursive words. I could not begin to be a professional speaker until I had mastered and figured out all there was to be a professional speaker. This metaphor of writing letters with an oversized pencil stopped progress dead in its tracks.

Done is better than perfect.
-Sheryl Sandberg

I don't want to leave you with the impression that working hard and striving for high standards is in anyway a bad thing. I am suggesting that sometimes perfectionism leads to procrastination. We put off executing an idea because we do not think it is ready yet or that we are ready yet.

I wanted to have all the answers and everything perfect before I began executing my plan of becoming a professional speaker. 20/20 hindsight shows me that in the end, perfection is not possible. We must take risks and learn from our mistakes. That is how we perfect our craft and our ideas.

It is when we replace perfectionism with progress that we begin to procrastinate. Using my example of handwriting, if all I did was perfect the perfect "A" I would have never progressed to other letters and eventually words.

Focus On Progress

When we look at progress as the gold standard rather than perfectionism, we begin to move forward on a consistent basis. Here is the funny thing about humans, we can lose momentum. We must keep our vision alive and we must have support and motivation.

Think about the brushing your teeth example. We may slack off for a time. But we know it is not right, but we fall out of the habit. It's not fun. It doesn't taste good. Orange juice becomes a nightmare after brushing our teeth. What happens the day before we go, or even an hour before we go to the dentist? We are brushing like mad. We are motivated and don't want any bad news. We want the dentist to say we are good brushers and our teeth look great. A week after we may slip back into the once a day brush. The point is we become motivated and our actions change.

When we break down our goals into small pieces, ones that we can see progress in daily, we move forward quicker. Remember what the real key was to brushing four times a day? Our parents, right? They checked our teeth and would ask us if we brushed. It was a daily goal that we were supported for and held accountable for. It got done.

If you are reading this book, more than likely you don't have a parent asking you daily if you brushed your teeth, did your homework and took out the trash. Well, you might have a spouse that does that. So maybe you need to take out the trash right now, I will wait for you right here. Stop putting it off.

STOP- READ- ACT

Hopefully, you took out the trash and maybe even brushed your teeth. Now I want you to take out a piece of paper and write some daily goals. Three, short goals. Put the list where you can see it. At the end of the day, I want you to review that list, and honestly answer the questions below. Write down your answers so that at the end of the week you can see how you progressed.

- ✓ Did you accomplish your goals?
- ✓ What were your strengths today?
- ✓ What were your weaknesses?
- ✓ What did you find interesting today?
- ✓ What opportunities did you miss?

I want you to focus on progress and success in small steps.

Eating The Elephant

There is the age-old question- How do you eat an elephant?

Answer- *One bite at a time.*

Breaking down larger goals into smaller ones, is an easier way to prevent procrastination and to experience more progress. You can celebrate smaller goals daily as you achieve them, rather than waiting months. We are motivated by success, even small ones.

Think about losing weight for a minute (I know many of you would rather not, but stick with me here). If you have a goal of losing 30lbs and you lose at the rate of a pound a week, you will be waiting at least 30 weeks (10 months) to achieve that goal. Most people quit, because they do not reach such a large goal soon enough. But if you pay attention and make daily and weekly goals for yourself, you will see the progress. If you set a goal of only eating a certain number of calories for the day and exercising for 20 minutes, then this is something you can immediately see progress on and achieve.

When we can see, and achieve progress on our goals, we are less likely to quit, less likely to procrastinate, because we can see progress. Before you know it, the elephant has been eaten, one piece at a time. (Yeah, the idea of eating an elephant is not a very pretty or appetizing metaphor for me either, but it is one that has been around awhile. If I had said giant cake instead of elephant, you might have figured out a way to eat it all in one session, and it would defeat the purpose of the metaphor. Therefore, we will stick with elephant. Bon appetite.)

Accountability

Later in the book, I will discuss the different personalities, but some people do better with the support of others. They can stay on track and procrastinate less when they have someone holding them accountable. A good accountability partner can help us create attainable goals, and hold us accountable to our commitments.

"Eric, I scheduled you for an appointment with the eye doctor today." This statement from my wife seemed insignificant at the time. Everything changed when the doctor reported that I had a detached retina and that if it was not treated, I risked blindness.

I had canceled the previously scheduled eye appointments, guilty of the very thing I speak about – procrastination. I didn't look forward to the long wait and uncomfortable eye exam, so it was easy for me to find reasons to put it off. Are there any uncomfortable tasks that you have been putting off that are vital to your success?

If you procrastinate for too long, it can cost you your vision. Not necessarily your physical eyesight, but your vision as it relates to your goals and dreams. So, how do you stay focused when the journey is uncomfortable?

Accountability – My wife is the ultimate accountability partner. If I have a doctor's appointment, I know that she will remind me about it beforehand, and ask me how it went afterwards.

Finding a like-minded accountability partner that you must answer to, will keep you on track. Once you have identified this person, pick a goal that is critical to your ultimate purpose. Then, communicate your goal to your partner and establish follow up timelines.

Hiring the right business coach can also keep you accountable. One of the biggest challenges with being an entrepreneur is not having a boss to hold your feet to the fire. A good coach can make you aware of your patterns of procrastination and provide you with someone to answer to.

Association – Make it a habit to have regular fellowship with groups of people that are on the same path as you. My involvement with the National Speakers Association keeps me accountable and helps me stay focused on my goals as a professional speaker.

If your goal is to grow as an entrepreneur, plug into your industry's association and commit to attending the meetings. I have found that attending the annual conventions will shorten your learning curve by as much as six months in comparison to not attending.

Many of these associations form "mastermind groups". This is a select group of people that meet on a regular basis for the sole purpose of sharing best practices and holding each other accountable.

The entrepreneurs and executives I have worked with report that finding the right mastermind group is a life changing experience.

Having an accountability system will help you to stay focused when the journey is uncomfortable.

STOP- READ- ACT

In his book, Think and Grow Rich, Napoleon Hill said the following "Every adversity carries with it the seed of an equal or greater benefit." The key to maintaining the right perspective on your failures is to focus on the lessons that you learned from it.

To accomplish this, I create a "lessons learned" list for any setback I experience. In the memo app on my phone, I notate all the positive lessons that resulted from a specific setback.

For example, when I competed in the Toastmaster's speech contests, any result less than a first-place finish was a setback for me. During those times that I finished short of my goal, I would write the positive lessons that I gained from the experience. I would notate things such as becoming a better story teller, and gaining valuable stage time as takeaways.

This habit helped me to move forward with the right attitude and perspective. If you discipline yourself to using the lessons learned list, you will maintain the right perspective and be less likely to procrastinate in the pursuit of your goals.

Right now, I want you to go on your computer or smartphone (come on I know you have one), and look for an app like Evernote ™ that can help you create a "lessons learned" list. Install it right now, and begin using it to record your daily lessons. This can be a part of the last action I asked you to perform.

Remember the rule- put the book down and do not open it again until you have completed the task. Go on--- get on your phone. No, no, no, don't check Facebook, find the app!

5

Impulsivity

A man's reaction to his appetites and impulses when they are aroused gives the measure of that man's character.
-David O Mckay

There is a war that is raging within each us. There is an urgency of NOW that is the core to this battle, which has two distinct, very different opponents.

In one corner weighing in at 175 lbs. is the progressive. This part of us knows what we need to be successful. It has a purpose and a plan.

In the other corner weighing in at 350 lbs., (and frankly weighing in to a lot of our decisions) is the procrastinator. This part of us puts things off until later and uses our fears, flaws and failures against us.

Here is a glimpse of a typical day of battling between these opposing sides of myself.

Morning- 4:30 AM
Progressive- My alarm goes off and as I hear it I am reminded that I had a goal to get up early to work out.

Procrastinator - I hit the snooze button. What will ten more minutes really matter? The sleep felt great, and I woke up in time to go to work. Two weeks went by and I still had not gotten up for a workout.
Score 1 for the Procrastinator.

Evening- 6:00 PM sharp
Progressive- This is the time my Toastmasters class begins. I want to learn more about professional speaking into order to improve and make it a career.

Procrastinator- I am tired. It has been a long day at work, and all I want to do is go home, sit in my chair and flip through Sportscenter on the TV. I am owed the time to relax and besides, what will one missed meeting really cost me. Three months later, I was still missing the weekly meetings.

Score another 1 for the Procrastinator.

Bedtime 9:00 PM

Progressive- I want to write a book. It is 2011 and this is my year to get it done. It is important for my career as a speaker and author.

Procrastinator- It is hard to write a book and get it published. What will one more day mean? It will get done. Eventually. In 2017, six years later I got it done.

Score another 6 for the Procrastinator, because that is how many years I put it off getting it done.

Subtle Compromises

Each of the stories above are real and each involve me making subtle compromises. I made quick impulsive decisions and gave into the procrastinator. These small compromises can become big issues and have a way of becoming a habit over time.

- ✓ If I leave a few minutes early from work, no one will notice.
- ✓ If I arrive a few minutes late to work, who is it really hurting.
- ✓ I can start my diet tomorrow.
- ✓ I can speed at least nine miles over the speed limit, I won't get pulled over.

Why do we make these compromises? It is a release from something unpleasant. If you don't like your job, you will not be motivated to be on time and want to stay. Therefore, we give into impulsivity, as it leads to an immediate release from feeling uncomfortable. Many times, the answer is to just put off the uncomfortable situation.

When we are bored with a task or not into it, then the beckoning of checking our emails, texting, looking at social media or even reorganizing our desks is an easy way out. A few minutes can turn into hours of procrastination and it becomes the norm.

The First Step is Awareness

One of the first steps in combating impulsive procrastination is to become aware of it. You must know that you are doing it and catch yourself. At the end of the chapter I have provided you an impulsivity test to give you an idea of how impulsive you might be.

Once you can see it, and identify when you are giving into procrastination, the easier it is to combat it. The truth is, we all do it, including yours truly. We are wired to find ways to lessen anxiety in our minds and body. It used to be running from a dangerous hungry bear, now it is about running away from a scary profit and loss report.

Do you remember the story about the frog in the pot of water? If you put a frog in a pot of hot water, it will immediately jump out of the pot. If, however, you put it in cold water and then gradually increase the temperature to boiling, you will have boiled frog. Yeah, I don't want that soup either.

When the frog is in the cold water, it will ignore the subtle changes in temperature. It might shift around a bit, but it won't jump out. It will make subtle compromises, but in the end, it will become soup no one will want to eat. Your dreams and goals can become just like that frog if you begin to make subtle compromises. Over time your dream becomes boiled and ruined.

You must be aware and pay attention to your choices, and ask yourself why you are making the decision and does it align with your goals.

Let's try a short Impulsivity Test- to determine your level of impulsivity.

Impulsivity Test

Take a piece of paper and number it 1-15. Read each of the questions below and answer with the first answer that comes to your head and mark it on your paper. Do not think about your answers too much, just move through the test quickly. There are no right or wrong answers.

1.   When someone suggests a new project, you...

   a.   Jump right in

   b.   Ask some questions first

   c.   Want more information and time to think about it

2.   When shopping you see something you like do you...

   a.   Buy it- maybe two of it if it comes in more than one color

   b.   Walk around the store first to see if there is something else you might like

   c.   Wait to go home and see if it is selling cheaper on line

3.   In a new relationship, you tend to...

   a.   Talk about moving in together by the third date

   b.   Take things a steady pace and allow the relationship to unfold naturally

   c.   Google them and do background checks on them- and check out their social media history

4. When buying a car, you…

    a. Buy the first thing you see on the lot

    b. Talk to the salesperson about several different options

    c. Do all of your research online before you ever go to the car lot

5. When choosing where to go for dinner you…

    a. Chose the place closest to where you are

    b. Talk over a few options

    c. Look online at menus and think about what you are hungry for

6. When you send an email, do you…

    a. Just hit send without scanning it for errors

    b. Read over it once before sending

    c. Let it sit awhile as a draft and think about it before sending

7. When you buy something from the store that requires assembly, do you…

    a. Forget the directions and jump in

    b. Have the directions open for reference

    c. Read through the directions a few times before getting started

8. When reading a book, do you…

    a.   Jump to the end to see what happens

    b.   Read quickly and skim some parts

    c.   Read it slowly word for word

9. When in a meeting do you…

    a.   Interrupt others before they end what they are saying

    b.   Listen to what others are saying but are writing down your questions

    c.   Listen to others, think about what they said, and ask for clarification

10. Do you…

    a.   Act before you think

    b.   Think before you act

    c.   Act only when you have all the facts

11. During the holidays or birthdays do you

    a.   Insist on opening presents- you hate to wait

    b.   You open your presents first

    c.   You wait until everyone has opened their presents before you open yours

12. At a stop do you…

    a.   Honk at a person that does not move immediately when the light turns green

    b.   Wait a few seconds to see if the person moves.

    c.   Wait as long as it takes

13. Do you find yourself…

    a.   Always in a hurry

    b.   Pressured to get things done

    c.   Never in a hurry, you take your time

14. Do you arrive…

    a.   Ahead of time

    b.   Just in time

    c.   When you get there- safety first

15. Do you often

    a.   Get speeding tickets

    b.   Try to watch out for police when driving fast

    c.   You just leave earlier and never speed

Tally up your answers. If most of your answers were "a" then you tend to be very impulsive. If your answers were mostly "b" you may be a little impulsive but you tend to get things done on time. If you answered "c" you are not impulsive, however you may be procrastinating and taking too long to get things accomplished in your day.

If you know the 'why', you can live any 'how'.
-Friedrich Nietzsche

The Secret Sauce

Some authors make you wade through an entire book to give you the one nugget that you need to succeed in your particular struggle. Lean in closer and pay attention, because I am going to give it to you right here. Why procrastinate and make you wait right?

You must know your WHY!

I mentioned purpose earlier in the book, and your Why is married closely to that concept. Your Why is your:

Mission

Meaning

Motive

Knowing your Why drives you beyond the self-imposed limitations you may have in your life. It essentially erases procrastination, as it becomes the central driver in all our decisions. How can you discover your Why? Your purpose defines your goals, your Why defines your actions.

STOP- READ- ACT

I want you to write down the following questions on a piece of paper, and then close this book. I want you to think hard about the answers and write them down. These are the answers that will become the drivers in every decision you make every day, so have them handy. If you are deciding, these can help you remain aligned with your purpose. The other thing that it does is forces you to stop and think about your actions, which then eliminates impulsive decisions.

- ✓ What are you passionate about?
- ✓ What does success mean to you?
- ✓ If you could make a difference to a person or cause what it be?

Write them down, think about them and write your answer. When you are done, open the book again.

I Know The Moment I Figured Out My 'Why'

It was May 4, 2010, at 12:39 PM, when I finally knew my Why. How could I possibly know that moment with such certainty? It was the moment my daughter was born.

I now had a family, and I needed to look beyond just my purpose, I had meaning, mission and motive. I had my Why. It was my family.

Morning Alarm Rings

I wake up and I get to my work out. I know my family relies on me to be healthy and fit so that I can provide and that I can be around to love and support them.

Evening Toastmasters Meeting

Sure, I am tired after a day's work, but I must stay true to my purpose, which is to be a professional speaker. My family relies on me to work toward a better future, and so I do what I must to ensure that happens.

The Book

Since you are reading this, you know that I eventually got off my duff and got it done. It was part of the greater goal of propelling my speaking business forward.

You need to find your Why to find and focus on your dreams. We are all prone to take the easy way, but there is no easy way, and that is what turns into impulsive action and compromises. When your Why is strong, you overcome the temptation to put off your dreams. You become focused and you begin every decision with - What is my Why?

STOP- READ- ACT

In the last chapter, I had you begin to write down your daily progress. Now I want you to look at your list of daily progresses over a week. I want you to begin to see trends and where you made compromises.

Write down what those compromises were, and more importantly how you intend to fix and avoid them in the future. Go on now, and do it. I will see you in chapter 6 when you are done.

6
Failing to Say 'No'

The essence of strategy is choosing what not to do.
-Michael Porter

It is important to know you purpose and your Why, but procrastination can drag you down, and as you have seen, it can come in many forms. In this chapter I am going to discuss the difference between busy-ness and business. You can be overwhelmed and be busy, but not take care of business. One of the greatest issues that creates busy-ness is the inability to say NO.

I'm reminded of a conversation I had with my friend, Lisa.

"Eric, you're always talking about time management. I need your help. I'm stressed out. I'm burnt out. I'm wearing a lot of hats. I got a lot of my shoulders. I really need your help."

"Ok, no problem, Lisa. What is your schedule for this coming Thursday at 6:00 p.m.? I'll talk to you at that time."

"Well, Eric. That's not going to work. You see, I'm the president of my PTA. We've got a meeting at that time," she replied

"Okay, no problem, Lisa. Well, what about that following Wednesday at 7:30 p.m.? I have an opening there," I said.

"Well, no, Eric, that's not going to work, either. I'm the Vice President of my Home Owner's Association. We've got a meeting at that time."

"Okay, not a problem. I see the weekdays don't work for you, so let's try Saturday at 2:00 PM," I offered.

"No, Eric. That's not going to work either. I'm planning the summer office social for my job, so that's not going to work."

Lisa's schedule was so loaded with meetings that she didn't even have time to address her time management issue. I asked myself, "How did

Lisa get into this position?" She failed to use the magic word. She hadn't learned to say "NO." I have a motto about that:

The More You Say Yes, The More You'll Have Stress.

The No List

Noted author Gary Ryan Blair came up with the concept of having a No List, where you proactively write down requests that, if they emerge in the future, you know to decline. Blair believes that the key to your success is to have a short "yes" list and a long No List.

The first item that you should have on your list is something that you're not passionate about. You should ask yourself the questions of what is your Why and Purpose. What is it you are passionate about?

If you feel like you're just saying "yes" out of obligation, chances are that it is something that belongs on the "no" list.

Next, you must identify your priorities. Therefore, I had you write down your purpose and your Why in previous chapters. You did not skip that, did you? That way, if a request comes across your desk that's not aligned with your purpose or Why, you automatically know to say "no".

The third key is to identify your personal capacity. You don't have the personal capacity to do the task, that should go on your "no" list. I find that in the work environment, it's dangerous to be known as someone that is very competent, because that's when you'll start receiving requests outside of your area. You can't take on all this extra responsibility. The person making the request may assume that because of your competence in other areas, you can fulfill their request with ease. You must know your abilities and limitations well enough to know when to say "no" to requests.

Whenever you say yes to a request you aren't passionate about, by default you are saying NO to one you are.

STOP- READ- ACT

It should be like a velvet rope. Only the most important chores and jobs get in, and the rest are turned away. It's important to have a block for those things that take up too much of your time from following your Why and Purpose.

I use something I call The Velvet Rope Test to determine if I should decline a request or not. To follow this test, you take the time to look at your passions, visions and goals and compare it to the request. Will fulfilling the request help you fulfill your own passion, realize your vision or reach your goals? If it doesn't fit in the lineup, then it goes into your "no" list.

List some of the jobs you have agreed to do in the past 6 weeks. These can be at work or at home. Now, take your purpose and your why documents and place them to the right of this piece of paper. These are your velvet rope. Place a clean piece of paper at the right of these papers, and right down which tasks make it across the rope.

Once you have done this, look at your list to see what is left. Is there any way you can delegate these tasks to others? Ok get to work.

Top 10 Reasons We Don't Say 'No'

When we say, we are busy all the time, we are putting off other tasks that may be as important as or more important than the ones we spend the most time putting our energy into. These are some reasons I have heard that you may find yourself saying. You must be aware of these warning signs to work through them.

- I will hurt someone's feelings.
- I should never pass on an opportunity.
- This will lead to something bigger.
- I got this. (No really you don't)
- One more thing can't hurt.

- If I don't do it, who will.
- This is a great honor to be asked.
- If I say no, they will never ask me again.
- I can find someone to help me.
- This won't impact my workload.

Learning How to Say 'No'

Believe it or not, you can say "no" while you're on the job. Even if your supervisor makes a request, you can still say, "no" if the task is outside of your abilities. Be tactful, of course. (Don't get yourself fired and then blame this chapter of the book!) I have made the following statement to supervisors in the past: "I am concerned that if I take on this project, my job performance will suffer and I will not be able to deliver the best service to my customers." Communicating this way sends the message that you are saying no to the request and not the person.

To be positioned, you must be positioned in your passions. Learn to say "no" when things don't help you pursue your passions, meet your priorities or fall within your personal capacity.

Has saying NO to a friend or associate ever left you feeling like a jerk? I have felt this way at times because I thought I was rejecting the person and letting them down. I now realize the importance of separating the request from the person.

Saying NO to the request will get you past the fears of letting people down, damaging relationships, and burning a bridge for future advancement. So how do you say NO to the request without regret? The following are my Three P's to an effective NO statement:

Positive Acknowledgement: Begin your no statement by positively acknowledging the person for thinking enough of you to ask. This is the first step towards declining the request and not the person. Some positive acknowledgements are "Thank you for thinking of me" or "Thank you for the offer."

Plainly Admit: In this phase, you plainly admit why you can't accept what's being offered. This lets the person know that you have another obligation or specific reason outside of them for not saying yes. If the only reason you are saying no is that you don't want to do it, you can say the following:

"This opportunity doesn't line up with my personal goals" Or "For personal reasons, I am not able to take this on."

Propose Alternatives: This step allows you to say NO and still be a resource for the requester. For example, if you are asked to chair a committee, you can recommend that they ask another person in the organization who may be just as qualified. It also helps to leave the door open for the future when you may be in a position to say yes. I recommend using the following question: "Can we reconnect on this later?" This keeps you from burning your bridges and helps to maintain a positive relationship.

Below are some scripted examples of how to use the Three P's

Unpaid Tutoring:

Thank you for thinking of me. Unfortunately, I have other commitments on my calendar that would keep me from taking on more. Can we talk again if my schedule changes?

Leadership roles:

Thank you for thinking of me. I have already committed myself to other projects and will not have the time to serve in the role. Have you considered asking _____? Please keep me in mind for this in the future.

Work Requests from Boss:

Wow, that's an interesting project. I am really busy with the XYZ assignment right now, so let me know if you want me to re-prioritize.

So, there you have it. Starting your statement with a positive acknowledgement, plainly admitting why you are saying no, and proposing alternatives, will allow you to say no without feeling like a jerk.

This is the end of Part One.
By now you should:

- Know Your Purpose
- Know Your Why
- Know the common causes of procrastination
- Know the negative effects of procrastination
- Have a working plan to become more focused and have an increased self-awareness.

If you don't know all of these, please review Part One before proceeding with the rest of the book.

Part Two
Don't Procrastinate Procrastination

In Part One of the book you learned about what procrastination is and what it can cost you in your life. None of us are immune to its influence in our lives, and so it takes a very conscious and willful strategy to overcome it. Face it, you cannot overcome a passive habit by being passive. This was one of the reasons I chose to write this book, because I found several well-meaning books on procrastination that point out what it is, and what potential issues it can cause, but that is where it stops.

Part Two is where you learn how to consciously look at your life, look at the obstacles you are facing concerning procrastination and most importantly, how to deal with it head on. The best way to deal with procrastination is to act immediately. In Part One, you should have begun to understand what that feels like by doing the Stop, Read, Act sections.

This part of the book takes it one step further. Now you will Assess, Plan, Act in each chapter.

Assess- At the beginning of each chapter are 5 simple questions. If you answer yes to one or more of them, that indicates that you must move to Plan and then Act. Each chapter is based upon my Procrastination Prevention Pyramid. More about that in moment.

Plan- You will find activities and plans of action to deal with whatever manifestation of procrastination you may be dealing with. Choose one quickly and move then to Act.

Act- Much like in Part 1, you must put the book down immediately and Act upon your chosen plan of attack. Attack is the best word because it indicates decisive action. Procrastination is a mighty and alluring foe, and so it will take all your will and inner resolve to overcome it.

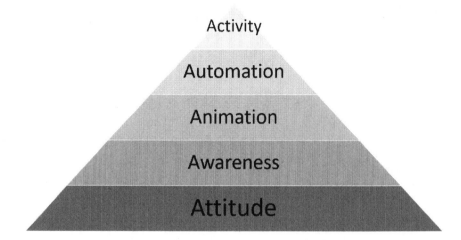

The Procrastination Prevention Pyramid

In the next five chapters I will describe to you the different levels of the Procrastination Prevention Pyramid. While teaching how to combat procrastination, I offered my audiences some specific strategies and over time I realized they fell into categories. I also realized that there were some foundational pieces which were important to consider first- namely attitude and mindset. Without the right mindset, you cannot hope to be able to alleviate the negative influence procrastination has on your life. I began stacking other categories with increasing action levels until I reached Activity at the top, the most active strategy.

There is not really a hierarchy, as much as foundational concepts that must be in place before the higher categories can be considered. It should be noted that you may jump around or even work at more than one level at a time to counteract procrastination. Therefore, I included five questions for each, so that you can determine at any time whether that is an area that needs work.

How To Use Part Two

In part one you learned the signs and consequences of procrastination. When you are feeling rushed, or are not being productive, and you are feeling like you can never get anything done, these are all signs that you may be dealing with procrastination.

Begin with chapter 7, and ask yourself the five questions. Pay attention to which questions you answer yes to - then stop, review the strategy and apply the action. If you are still struggling, go to the next level and the next and repeat the process. You may find yourself applying multiple strategies from different levels. That is because no one person's situation is the same as another's. No one handles procrastination the same way, and therefore sometimes it takes some experimenting to find the right combination.

An important rule to remember is to act immediately. Don't put it off- just do it right now. If you find yourself hesitating it may be time to challenge your mindset. Are you ready to let go of procrastination in your life? What are the excuses you are coming up with? Write them down and really assess if they are valid excuses.

If there are legitimate reasons you are not acting immediately you have a couple of options. Either remove what it is blocking you, or try a new strategy. Keep trying and working at it until you find a strategy that works.

7
Attitude

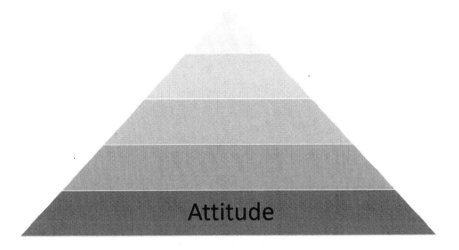

Assess

Respond to the five questions below either yes or no. If you answer yes to any of them, then continue to the Plan and then Action.

- I believe that I don't have enough time during the day to accomplish my priorities.
- When speaking about my career or business, I focus more on what's going wrong than what's right.
- I believe that I have been the victim of bad luck
- When running late, I tend to blame traffic
- I have a mental picture of myself as being a chronic procrastinator.

The way we see the world, more specifically "our world", affects our attitude, mood and ultimately outcomes in our lives. That is why it is essential to have the right mindset and attitude before attempting to tackle procrastination.

It has been shown that negative thoughts can lead to procrastination. Negative thoughts are normal, and in fact many of the thoughts that float about our mind are just that- negative. Why?

As I mentioned in Part 1, our reptilian brain is the part of our mind that keeps us safe, and is constantly scanning our environment. It is looking for things that could harm us and may push us into a flight or fight situation. This means we are constantly looking for problems.

Teachers in classrooms spend an inordinate amount of time, especially in certain grades, dealing with discipline problems. In fact, they could spend up to 80% of their time addressing it, which leaves very little time for teaching. Research has shown that concentrating on negative behaviors, and using disciplinary actions, does not work, and can have the negative effect of creating helplessness in students. We will talk about that in a minute.

What has been found to be effective, is to apply a reward when students do things correctly. At first, this can be awkward for a teacher, but with some practice, it becomes the new "normal" way of looking at their classroom. The results are that the teacher spends more time teaching and the mood of the classroom is focused on success rather than failure. In addition, the students feel more confident and motivated to be rewarded. It is a system that works.

Learned Helplessness

When we feel like no matter what we do we will not succeed, we have embraced learned helplessness. Procrastination thrives where learned helplessness exists because if it does not matter what we do, why even try?

There was a study in which fish were placed in a tank, and a glass wall was inserted. On the other side of the wall was food. The fish tried to get to the food, and bonked their little heads every time. When the wall was removed and the food was dropped into the same location, the fish did not move. They had learned that it was no use trying, since there was an invisible force ready to impede their progress. So, they just swam on and gave up.

During the barbaric times of training elephants for circuses, young elephants were trained to remain in place, by placing a chain around their leg, tied to a stake in the ground. When they were small, they did not have the strength to pull the stake up or break the chain. As they grew, the chain was placed on their leg, but they never tried to pull loose, even though they could. They had adopted learned helplessness.

We are not fish nor elephants, but we can easily fall into a similar mindset. You are not good enough for a better job. Not smart enough for school. Not pretty enough to date. Enough with the enough. Learned helplessness can be crippling, so when you recognize it in yourself, you must be aware that this exists inside of you. It is a fantasy we create, but none of it is real. Time to rip back the veil and concentrate on your purpose and your "why". You are in control.

Don't Become the Label- Unless it is a Positive One

If I am guilty of making you feel bad about being a procrastinator, let me apologize. That is not my intention. My purpose is to make you aware so that you can take greater control over the times you do procrastinate. Don't take on the label, because this can have the effect of you becoming the label. We are what we think we are, or at least we can create what we think we are. That power can be used to create something greater.

Everyone creates labels to help categorize and make sense of their world. Why not choose labels that are positive? Success. Pioneer. Innovator. Leader. Doer. Producer.

Be aware of your language. Are the words mostly positive? How do you refer to yourself? Are they positive attributes? Self-deprecation can be a way to be humble or in some situations humorous. It can also be a problem when it is used often.

"Oh, I can't do that, I'm not smart enough."

"If it weren't for bad luck, I would not have any luck at all."

"Only people at a higher pay grade than me can make a decision concerning that."

Gratitude

One of the most effective ways to switch the negative programming that goes on in our heads is to practice gratitude. That is to acknowledge and appreciate all the positive things in our lives. It is an even greater more expansive practice when we can show gratitude for others around us. It raises our consciousness into a positive mindset.

I served as mentor for a gentleman, let's call him Bob. Bob was struggling in his business and even in his home life. Whenever I spoke with Bob, he told me all about how his business was not working, and that he was ready to give up. No matter what he tried, he could not get his numbers up. When he went home, his negative outlook affected his relationship with his wife.

I asked Bob to tell me something he was thankful for. He struggled a bit with this question, and could not immediately come up with an answer. I gave him homework to be prepared for the next time we spoke. He had to tell me five things he was thankful for.

A week went by and when we spoke he was prepared. I made it a standing order that every time we spoke he had to tell me what he was thankful for. Even when we began talking and I saw him slipping back into a negative, helpless talk, I brought him back around to things he was thankful for.

His business picked up. It was a breakthrough for him and things continued to grow all because his mindset changed. Even his marriage had improved with the gratitude mindset.

Now that you have an understanding about how attitude and mindset can affect your level of procrastination, it is time to do something about it.

Plan

Each day I use a 3" x 5" index card to write down everything that I am focused on for that day. On the front, I have my daily goals. These are the tactical to-do items that will help me achieve my strategic 12 month goals.

On the back of the card, I write down the things for which I am thankful. Areas such as my health, family, and friendships rank high on the list. As I experience failures and setbacks, reflecting on my goals and what I am grateful for allows me to maintain the right perspective.

I like the 3 x 5 Card because it fits neatly in my shirt pocket and I can carry it wherever I go. The card is sturdy enough to allow me to write while in the palm of my hand, which allows me to make changes if I am not around a hard writing surface.

Act

Begin by telling those around you how much you appreciate them and what they mean in your life. Do it now. Call them. Text them. Email them. Send a raven with a note attached to its leg. Just close this book and act.

8
Awareness

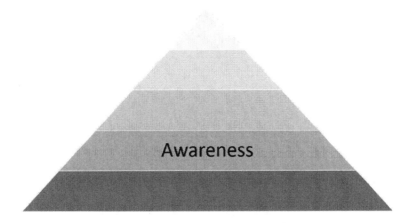

What is necessary to change a person is to change his awareness of himself.

- Abraham Maslow

Assessment

Respond to the five questions below either yes or no. Pay close attention to those you answer yes to as you move to the next section.

- I am aware of my personality tendencies and how they relate to my procrastination habits.
- I am aware of the times of day when I have the most energy and schedule my tasks accordingly.
- My environment is organized to maximize my productivity and minimize distractions.
- I spend a minimum of 5 hours per month networking with like-minded people.

- I only seek advice from those who have achieved the results I desire in the specific area I have questions about.

Having a keen awareness of those around you, your environment and your general response to that environment can greatly impact your level of procrastination. When you lack awareness of what is going on in your life that is leading to reduced productivity, then it can be rather difficult to fix. In this section, you will learn your style of interaction, your daily rhythms and environmental issues that can make finishing tasks in a timely manner difficult and in some cases impossible.

DiSC Assessment

I could write a book about DiSC and the wonderful things it can teach you, however, I would likely get in a bit of trouble over copyright issues, and worse it would not be useful within the confines of this book. DiSC is an assessment you can take that helps you visually see what type of person you are when it comes to working with others. There are DiSC assessments that will also give you a composite of how you and your boss are compatible and areas in which you can adjust your style.

Procrastination Styles

Once you have determined your style you can then reference in this section how it affects your tendencies toward procrastination.

A common recipe for failure is the mixture of the right idea with the wrong plan. Recently, I was unable to sleep because of nasal congestion and sneezing. To find relief I took some cold and flu medicine. The medication did not help, so I visited my doctor. The doctor told me that I had seasonal allergies; not a cold. He then prescribed a specific remedy based on my situation. As it turns out, I had the right idea, but the wrong plan.

Your desire to stop procrastinating on important tasks is the right idea. The fact that you continue in this habit is an indication that you have the wrong plan. What can be done to put the right plan in place?

Procrastination is nothing to take lightly. Having the right prescription based on your personality will help you to break the habit!

Your personality is a blend of genetic and learned tendencies. There are four types of procrastinators which correlate to the four personality types suggested in a DiSC assessment. You can match your type below to the procrastination type. The DiSC assessment places you on a grid in which you may be of a certain type, and in some cases, you may be a combination of two. The same is true of procrastination types, therefore it is important that you review each one to determine which type fits you best.

Below is a breakdown of these areas along with a procrastination prescription that is specific to each type:

1. Driver Dan **(D)** – Dan is the "type A" personality. He is driven, results focused, confrontational and assertive. Michael Jordan and Tom Brady would be good examples.

Drivers tend to respond to deadlines, so if this sounds like you, the best way to overcome procrastination would be to make sure you give yourself a firm deadline for completion. Drivers do not do well with deadlines in the far future, as they tend to take these less serious. Creating more immediate deadlines motivates them to work harder.

They tend to take the attitude of - "You are not in charge of me."

This was true with a family of business owners that I know of. It was parents and two children running the company, and each of them were drivers. Whenever an idea came up for discussion, it was a mess because each of them did not want the other telling them what to do. As soon as a person came up with an idea or solution, the rest would automatically try to shoot it down. I can imagine what picking a restaurant to eat at must have been like for this family.

They hired a coach who helped them develop strategies to make each of them feel like they had ownership of ideas, so that they could work together and reduce conflict.

I admit I am a Driver Dan. I must discipline myself when it comes to long projects. For instance, this book. Do you know it took me three weeks just to write this paragraph?

My strategy is to create a daily goal, one that I can meet. In the case of writing, I block off one hour each day using a kitchen timer. Having a daily deadline forces me to make the most of the time.

2. *Sanguine Sally* (i) – Sally thrives off being the center of attention and loves to hear her own voice. She lives for the here and now and likes to have fun. Kim Kardashian and Dennis Rodman come to mind when I think of a Sanguine.

A Sally will procrastinate most on tasks that are not perceived to be fun and enjoyable.   Creating a reward system for accomplishing the objective is a way around this. Pair a reward with something you are not motivated to do, like pair a glass of wine with doing the dishes. Before you know it, you will be doing the dishes and singing, and laughing. If you are a Sally, treating yourself to a weekend getaway as a reward for finishing that business plan will help you move forward.

3. *Analytical Al* (S) – Al likes to have all the facts and details in order before he acts. Engineers and accountants tend to have this type of personality. The movie character "Dr. Emmett Brown" from *Back to the Future* fits the description.

An Al's tendency is to be slow in making decisions when the next steps are not concrete. This can lead to paralysis by analysis. This person tends to use "what if.." a lot to continue their analysis, but they rarely get out of the starting gate. They delay action through over analysis. Having the plan written out in detail before you proceed will lessen the chance of procrastination.

Al's tend to give more credibility to things in writing, so make sure they have it in writing.

If you are writing a book, having the title, chapters and talking points for each chapter written out in advance would be a great way to start.

4. Peacemaker Patricia (C) – Patricia likes to see everyone get along, avoids confrontation and does not want to make waves. She is agreeable and easy to like. "Mr. Rogers" of *Mr. Rogers Neighborhood* would be an example.

Patricia's like doing tasks that are easy, and get overwhelmed by those that seem complex. Their natural response to a complicated assignment is to do nothing.

If you are a Pat, breaking the task down into specific action steps, and committing to one step at a time will make things easier. You must ask yourself: "What is the next step?"

Pat's have the hardest time forming habits and maintaining routines because they lack internal motivation. Making goals public would be helpful. Having external accountability coming from a coach, accountability partner, or a mastermind group is the key.

If you are writing a business plan, focus all your initial attention on the first step of creating a vision statement. Focusing step-by-step will be easier for you than looking at all the details of the project.

Power Times (Lark or Owl)

Do you work better at night or during the day? This is important to know, as it will drive what job and shift you take. We each have a certain alert and sleep cycle our bodies follow. Knowing when you work the best will help you prioritize your day and reduce procrastination. You should schedule high priority activities during your high-energy times when possible. When you are at your low energy period, you are more likely to become unfocused and unproductive.

This is not always possible, and so sometimes you must be creative. I am an early Lark. I work the best when the sun is rising, not setting. However, sometimes my speaking engagements are at night, when my energy is lower, so I take natural supplements and an energy drink during these times for a boost. The important thing is to be aware of your energy fluctuations and prepare for them ahead of time. I sometimes make the mistake of waiting until the end of the day to work on writing projects, which is the worst time for me. The result is that I will find other things to do and become unfocused. Does this sound familiar?

Distractors

You should be hyper aware of your environment and what is a booster and what is a distractor. Some people enjoy listening to music when they work, for some people it is a distraction. Some types of music can be distracting.

Be aware of all your senses and how they are influenced by your environment.

Sound- I have already mentioned music, but what other sounds are there in your environment? Are people asking you questions constantly? Do you hear other noises that are driving you nuts? Is the environment too loud? Too quiet? Sit and listen and be aware of the sounds in your environment. If they are distracting you can purchase noise cancelling headphones or a white noise machine.

Sight- What can you see? Is there enough light? Too much light? Are the colors of the walls too bright? Too busy? How about pictures around you? Neutral colors and simple patterns are the easiest and least distracting. Also, what are you looking at online? This is huge. Turn off that social media. There are programs that will lock it during working hours so that there is the least amount of distraction.

Smell- Do you smell food constantly? Are there other strong odors or even perfumes that are distracting you? Our sense of smell can affect our mood and concentration. For some people, certain essential oils can help them concentrate. You can buy a simple diffuser for your Lavender or orange essence.

Taste- If you are hungry when you are working, it can be very hard to concentrate. Know your eating patterns. Eat light meals when working as heavy ones can make you sluggish. Keep high protein/low carb snacks close as these can help you between meals and assist in keeping you alert.

Touch- Is your workplace comfortable? How about your chair? Your desk height? Do you need a pad for your wrists? Muscle pain and fatigue can be very distracting. Make sure your desk chair is the right height and that you move around during the day. I will discuss exercising later, but moving around helps reduce muscle and back problems as well as pumping blood to the brain and helps you stay focused. Have a reminder on your watch or phone to get up and move periodically.

Plan

The best advice I ever received was from my mother. She told me, "Birds of a feather flock together." This is so true of procrastinators. Be aware of who is around you. Are they productive people, or procrastinators? If you have ever tried to lose weight you know it is hard if you are the only one in your family or group of friends doing it. How are you going to eat the rabbit food on your plate across from someone eating a juicy burger?

The same is true of procrastinators. If you spend enough time around three procrastinators, you will become the 4th. We are terrible at enabling others around us to be procrastinators. That is why coaches of all sorts are essential for some of the tougher goals in our lives. Many people on January first take the tour of a new gym. They are shown how to use all the machines. You know you must get on the machines a few times a week, and get sweaty and sore to build a body. There is little mystery to the process. So why isn't everyone fit and in shape? Mostly, it's because it is not always much fun to do. So, procrastination begins to settle in. You skip sessions, you shorten them, you get frustrated that you did not lose 20 pounds in a month and you eventually stop going.

This is what personal trainers are for. They motivate and hold you accountable to your fitness goals. It is harder to make up excuses to a coach then it is to a gym that can't talk back.

Refer to the personality styles above. Some are prone to need more external motivation such as an accountability partner or a coach. Flock around people that are committed and demonstrate success and you are more likely to stay on track and not procrastinate as much.

Action

Get on the computer right now and look up Meetup (Meetup.com) groups and other accountability groups. Research mastermind groups in your area or even virtual ones. Invest the time, effort and expense in yourself. Send messages and introductions to at least three. Go on. Get searching!

9
Animation

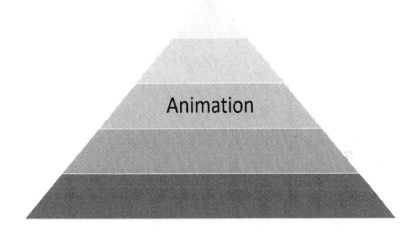

Assessment

Respond to the five questions below either yes or no. If you answer yes to any of them, then continue to the Plan and then Action.

- I exercise aerobically a minimum of four days per week.
- I get a minimum of seven hours of sleep each night
- I go to bed at a set time every night.
- I have a system in place to manage stress
- I have a daily habit of eating healthy food that boosts my energy levels.

How important is exercise, diet and sleep to success? It is estimated that 76% of wealthy people exercise at least four days a week, while 24% of those considered poor exercise only once a week. Motivated now?

Plan

Do you know which activity people procrastinate the most on?
Exercise.

Do you know what activity can help you battle procrastination at a physical level?

You got it- exercise.

Which comes first? The lack of exercise leads to procrastination, or procrastination leads to a lack of exercise.

Like most other concepts, I have covered in this book, there is a certain amount of mindfulness and will that occurs when trying to establish a new habit.

Exercise is not an activity that many enjoy. Why is that? Probably because sweating, groaning, and some days tying your shoes, can feel like you are attempting to climb Mount Everest.

There are many benefits of exercising such as improved overall health and fitness. It reduces the risk for certain serious health problems, and it also helps reduce procrastination as I have mentioned.

When we exercise, hormones called endorphins, which are happy chemicals, are released into our bloodstream. We become more motivated and energized. When we do aerobic exercises, those that increase our heart rate, we increase blood flow and therefore oxygen to our brains. This increases our ability to focus and be creative.

I am not an exercise scientist, and this is not an exercise manual. I do know that the more you exercise, the greater the benefits. But how can you get around the inevitable procrastination that plagues many of us when we look over at a treadmill?

Fun

Technology has made it possible for us to exercise just about anywhere these days. In addition, there are all kinds of gadgets that help increase the fun factor. Smartphones, fitness watches and even devices that can be inserted in a shoe, have turned the sometimes-laborious tasks into adventures.

Zombie Run ™ is an app that integrates running with a story line of running from Zombies. When they get closer you run faster or you lose some of your gear. There are many other of these types of story related apps that can be used while exercising.

There are all sorts of apps that help you monitor your progress and some that allow you to compete with others. I use the Nike+ app. I can see my friend's daily progress and they can see mine. Since I am a driver personality, if I see one of my friends ran two miles more than I did, I will hurry home and jump on the treadmill and beat them. They do the same until we just can't run anymore.

For the peacemaker personality, there are now apps that bring personal trainers to your home when even if they live hundreds of miles away. They do this via video. No more excuses. No more procrastination.

An analytical person may need something more visual to prompt them to exercise. They may need to prepare the night before by laying out their workout clothes, so in the morning the visual prompt will get them ready to exercise. Analytical personalities will benefit from written diet plans and tracking their calorie intake.

Sanguines like things to be fun so combining exercise with your favorite music can help. Listening to an entertaining audio book can be helpful as well.

Sleep Habits

In the last chapter I discussed Larks and Owls. Research shows that Owls have the hardest time with procrastination, especially in the business sector, because it is an early world. If you are required to get up and think early in the morning, and you are an Owl, you must make a concerted effort to shift your sleeping habits. It can take a while, because our habits are often biological in nature. There is a clock inside our brains that must be reset, so it takes time and persistence to affect a real change.

One way you can help yourself do this is to set an alarm to remind you to go to bed on time. Establish a nighttime ritual around bedtime that you repeat. Be sure that you stick to it, and over time, your sleeping habits will begin to change.

One of the toughest things on the body is to constantly shift your sleeping patterns. Doctors, especially those who are residents know how this can be. The reality is that our body requires proper sleep for healing, and transferring short term memory into long term memory. The lack of sleep can even lead to mental health issues like depression, and psychosis. Think about what I am saying here, and sleep on it.

Diet

For many, diet is a four-letter word. It is full of emotional triggers and is something people can battle their entire lives. Our weight is not only determined by environmental factors such as exercise, and nutrition, but it is also regulated by genetics. I do not bring up the idea of diet to trigger feelings of guilt associated with weight or body image. What I am referring to is the mind fuel you are putting into your body.

When you buy a brand-new car and you pull up to a gas pump for the first time, you may put high octane gas in. It can be as much as $0.60 more per gallon, but we want to put in the best and highest energy fuel possible, because we care about the car that we just signed our life over to get.

When you begin to understand that our bodies are machines, you will realize that the fuel that we put into it, has an impact on performance. Again, I am not a nutritionist, but I am someone who cares what fuels I put into my tank, because I want to be alert, healthy, and energized during my day.

When you put food with a lot of fat, sugar, or preservatives in it, you slow down the body. It can make you sluggish, because these toxic foods are hard to digest and process. Have you ever driven a car that needs a tune up? It can also be sluggish and make knocking sounds.

When we eat foods that overburden our metabolism, we have a hard time concentrating, and we can become tired. Fresh fruits and vegetables, lean meats, and even nuts can be high energy foods. Our body burns them quicker and more efficiently.

That is one of the secrets of eating to avoid procrastination. Eat smaller, more frequent meals. Since our body burns healthy foods quicker, we must fill the tank more often, but we must be careful of overeating as this will be a formula for nap time.

Knowing your personality type can be helpful. If you are a peace maker type, you may need a coach or a group to stay on track. There are organizations that have meetings such as Weight Watchers that can hold us accountable to what we eat. There are also many apps and online options just for exercising. There are scales to weigh yourself and record your progress.

Sanguines procrastinate most on those tasks they perceive to be laborious and monotonous. Give yourself a fun reward for achieving your dieting goal.

Drivers form habits easily and can easily form bad eating habits. Removing temptations from the environment would be helpful.

Analytical individuals will also benefit from online workout plans that line up with their goals since they thrive off structure and specific details. If their goal is to run a marathon or lose weight, there are workout plans they can access on line. For example, halhigdon.com has free online training plan for those interested in running a half or full marathon.

The important thing to remember is that you must plan. Nothing I have mentioned in this chapter is fun (at least not for many people) and so you must figure out what will work for you and motivate you to get started. Once you become healthy and clear headed, you will procrastinate less which means you will exercise and adhere to a diet and bedtime more consistently- the chicken and egg situation will be solved.

Action

Get online or go to an electronics store and explore the technology available to help make exercise more fun.

Find an app to help you monitor food and try it out for a week.

Set an alarm on your phone to let you know it is bed time.

Log what you ate today. Is it healthy? Did you eat for convenience or was it planned?

10

Automation

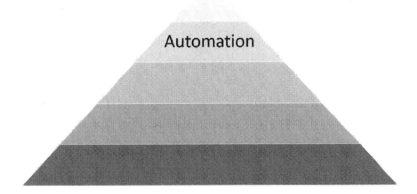

Assessment

Respond to the five questions below either yes or no. If you answer yes to any of them, then continue to the Plan and then Action.

- My email inbox only contains messages that I have yet to read.
- I have calculated the per hour value of my time.
- When delegating, I match the requirements of the job to the abilities of the person.
- I don't have any items "on my plate" that should be delegated.
- I use modern technology to maintain the right habits.

Plan

We live in a society much different than the one I grew up in. Kids today cannot imagine a world without the internet, smartphones, and computers. Even though our day to day lives have changed at an accelerated rate, our ability to process information has not increased.

Technology has grown to help automate our lives, but it is a double-edged sword in that it allows enormous amounts of data to barrage our mind daily. The result is a mental fatigue which unchecked can lead to procrastination, because our minds cannot process so much information and make decisions when it is overloaded.

In Kelly McGonigal's book *The Willpower Instinct*, she states that there is a negative correlation between the number of decisions we make every day and the quality of those decisions. We begin to become fatigued the more decisions we make and our willpower is weakened.

There are studies that show that a parolee is more likely to get a positive decision from a Judge in the morning, then they are at lunchtime or at the end of the day.

Have you ever asked your significant other where they want to eat on a Friday night after a long day of work? If they are like me, they don't want to make one more decision. Of course, if I abdicate my decision to my wife, I must live with her decision and love it, if I know what is good for me.

Retailers rely on your decision fatigue. Have you ever gotten to the checkout line and see all the candy bars, and toys just waiting for you? If you have a child, you know what is going to happen. Your willpower is weakened, and even though you never intended to by that Snicker's bar, you are paying for one just the same.

When we are overcome with decision fatigue, we are more likely to procrastinate on tasks we are not motivated to do. We say to ourselves that we will do it later or tomorrow. You are tired and you just don't want to do it. As I have said before, "later" and "tomorrow" rarely ever happen.

Self-Awareness

Knowing your limitations is important. You should be aware of when you are over extending yourself, because this can lead to bad decision making and procrastination. When I was a district manager I was responsible for 17 managers at different automotive service facilities. My personal motto was- Nobody Can Do It Better Than Eric. This was a trap that I had laid for myself, because every customer service complaint that came in, I was then dealing with. It wore me down, and I began slipping when it came to other duties, because I was fatigued. I was putting off what I needed to do, because I had placed myself in the position to make too many decisions.

One day I mercifully woke up to my self-imposed plight and told my managers, "If it gets to me, it's free. "

I did not care what it cost, I was going to give the customer back their money if I had to make the decision. I would not negotiate, and I would not spend any time working on it. Something miraculous happened.

My managers began handling the situations themselves in much the same way I had been handling them. They made better decisions and I became confident in their abilities. I was then able to get back to the priorities of my position that I had been procrastinating, and my decision fatigue all but vanished.

Being self-aware is a great thing. You will not make your best decisions when you are tired and mentally fatigued. Take short breaks and walk around (exercise even). Take that vacation you have been putting off until you retire or die- whichever comes first. Taking breaks keeps your mind fresh, motivated, and less prone to procrastination.

If you have ever taken a long trip, you know how your mind can wander. You can drive hundreds of miles and not even recall a trip, and this can be a dangerous thing because you can lose focus and your decision and reaction times can become impaired. This is why there are many regulations concerning on the road time for truck drivers.

Abdication and Delegation

Another way in which you can reduce your fatigue, especially in a management roll, is to learn to delegate. In my example above, I was surely not delegating in the beginning. Many people fall into the trap that no one can do as good a job as they can. When you have a team, you trust and have properly vetted and trained, then it is essential that you learn to let go and delegate.

The easiest things to delegate are things that you are not good at. As a driver, I tend to delegate administrative tasks such as finances and bookkeeping. Anything related to being detail oriented are tasks that I hand off to other people to help me with- I delegate, but I do not abdicate.

Abdicating means giving up the task entirely to someone else. This is when things can go sideways. If something goes wrong and the task is not done, you may still be responsible for the outcome. Instead, I delegate with follow-up. I check in on a regular basis to make sure tasks are being completed and to answer any questions others may have. These check-ins are usually short 20 minute, one on one meetings weekly.

Forming New Habits

As I have said earlier, change is hard, but the outcomes can be game changing.

It is estimated that 40% of what we do daily is habitual. When we can automate our day, we must make fewer decisions. This is one of the purposes of technology and innovation- to make our lives more automated and require us to make repeated decisions less often.

Have you ever noticed when ordering a pizza online it will ask you if you want to save your order for future purchases? You can just click a button the next time you want to order out, and it will fulfill your regular order- no real thought involved. There are all sorts of devices that can order items on a regular basis without much input from you. From razors to coffee, items can just appear on your doorstep like magic when you run out. The idea of course, that you will have more time to make more important decisions and therefore focus your life.

There are other ways in which you can add automation to your life. Some people have several matching suits or outfits in their closet. They do not have to think about what to wear in the morning, they can just reach in the closet and go. If you want more variety in your clothing choices, you may want to consider picking out your clothes before you go to bed. That way, when you are thinking about 10,000 things in the morning while getting ready for work, your clothing choice does not have to be one of them.

Many private schools adopted uniforms a long time ago. Now more and more public schools have adopted the practice. It is easier on the student to just wear the same clothes every day, as it is one less distraction and creates a more even playing field socially.

To create new habits, sometimes new triggers can be helpful. These are gentle reminders that help us through our day. For instance, I use an app that sends me reminders of what I have coming up in a text message. I can set it once and every day or on a certain day of the week, it will send me a reminder. This helps me unload that from my brain as something I must remember. I enter it once and it reminds me.

One of the triggers that I try to use and send reminders to myself are questions. One that I use with myself is, "Did I do my best to be on-time with every call today?"

I am a stickler about being on time and when I have back to back calls some days, I must try harder to be on task on those calls and not go over and procrastinate on time.

I use other apps to help me organize and prioritize my emails. Emails can be time killers and really lead to decision fatigue if we must deal with them all at once. I have certain folders that emails are automatically placed in depending on the person sending them. This way I can deal with the emails in an orderly fashion when I am ready to deal with them.

If you use social media in your business, you know what a time drain this can be, and sometimes you must think many times a day about what to write. I recommend using an app called HootSuite™. This service allows you to create social media blasts all at once to be delivered on the schedule you choose. You can spend an hour on a Sunday evening and have all your social media blasts setup for the week. I still respond to events that come up during the week when they happen, but for the most part, I allow Hootsuite to take care of the rest.

Action

Look for some Automation Apps available for your phone and try one or two out.

Create three questions to ask yourself that can be used as triggers for better habits.

Make a list of five things you can delegate and next to each write who can take over that task and how you intend to follow up.

11
Activity

Activity

Assessment

Respond to the five questions below either yes or no. If you answer yes to any of them, then continue to the Plan and then Action.

- I use a written to- do list every day.
- I prioritize what I do every day based on level of importance.
- I have written goals in place with set timelines for accomplishment.
- I have a system in place to review my daily and weekly activities.
- I have a note taking system in place to help me execute the good ideas I receive from books or other people.

Plan

33% of people plan their day and only 10% actually follow through with their plan.
-John Maxwell

Sometimes the prevention of procrastination is a feat of reverse engineering. We must determine how we are putting our goals into action and whether they are the most effective solutions.

What we have done in our past is the best predictor of our future. When we are ready to make actionable changes in our lives, whether it is building our business, creating a new sales stream, or finding a new company to work for, it is best we have a strategy for success so that we don't waste time in the process.

The best strategy for achieving a goal is to do enough of the right thing. When we do not achieve a goal it is often because of two issues:

Doing a lot of the wrong thing.

Not doing enough of the right thing.

Suppose you have the perfect resume, but you are only sending one or two a day out to prospective companies. This may be a case of not doing enough of the right thing. Conversely, suppose you are sending out thirty resumes a day, but it is out of date and has a bunch of typos. This is doing a lot of the wrong thing. In both cases, you would have difficulty achieving your goal of finding a new job.

Worse, you are wasting time. Either you are not spending enough time, and therefore procrastinating. Or, you may feel that your resume is so awesome that it is just a matter of days or hours before someone will read it and offer you a job of a lifetime. This is just lazy.

On the other hand, you are just wasting time peddling a resume no one will ever take seriously. Here is a serious question. Do you think that getting on a treadmill on the lowest setting will achieve your fitness goals even if you are on it an hour at a time? Or do you think that interval training (fast and then slow) for thirty minutes will have greater results. It is all about the numbers.

Know Your Numbers

The strategies in this chapter are about knowing your numbers. The number I am referring to is how many times you need to repeat a behavior daily to achieve a certain goal. This is a process of breaking a big goal, into smaller pieces, but in a way that is measurable and observable.

Let's use the example of sending out your resume. Suppose you want to obtain a new position at a new company, what will it take to land one? You must reverse engineer what it took for you to get the job you have now.

New Job	Hot Lead	Warm Lead
2 Hot Leads	10 Warm Leads	20 Applications

If you know that it takes at least two hot leads to get a new job then you can use the data above to figure out how many applications it will take to do it.

1 Hot Lead takes 200 applications. (20 x 10). So, you know that it will take twice that, or 400 applications to achieve your goal. If you want to land that new position in a month, this means you must be sending at least 20 applications a day, 5 days a week. Now you know your numbers for this goal.

Suppose that you want to get a position in two weeks. If you use the same process you can expect to send 200 applications a week. That is a lot of applications. You will reach your limit quickly and so you will need to make a change in your numbers. You will need to figure out how to reduce the number of applications needed to get a new job, rather than just filling out more applications. You must improve your process.

The important thing to figure out is your numbers. Then set up your daily schedule to accommodate your numbers.

Reassess

Once you have set up your daily routine around your numbers, it is important to reassess your progress. I have already mentioned, sometimes it is not about doing more of a behavior, it could mean you need to do something better.

In the case of sales calls, you may want to reduce the number of cold calls needed to create a warm lead. This may take some serious thinking, and implementation of a new strategy. After you implement that new strategy, you will need to reassess progress after a week or two and again make necessary changes. The main thing is not to become passive - you must actively look at your strategies to improve.

In school, we learned that the quickest route between two points is a straight line. It would be great if we could create a straight line to our goals, but this journey is like driving and flying.

Pilots adjust all the time when they fly. They don't fly straight from one place to the other. There are many micro-adjustments that must occur. All sorts of things pull a plane one way or the other, and then there is the fact that the Earth is also moving beneath the flying plane.

Can you remember the first time you drove? Your movements were stiff and you often over compensated in turns. Over time you began to drive much smoother, but you are constantly (more automatically) adjusting the steering wheel.

This same thought process goes into reaching goals. You must adjust while on your path. If you don't you can find yourself in a ditch. Procrastination, is like falling asleep at the wheel. When we hit something hard, we wonder how it happened, because we were not alert and paying attention. You must assess how you are moving through your days to reach your goals quickly and efficiently and avoid potholes along the way.

Feedback Loop

One of the ways you can be sure you remain on target and are not falling asleep at the wheel is to commit to a daily assessment of your progress.

You should ask yourself the following questions:

- ✓ What was positive about my day?
- ✓ What was interesting about my day?
- ✓ What was negative about my day?

You can write down your answers. If nothing else, it focuses you on what you need to do the next day. If you do record your responses you will begin to see patterns that you can then target to work on and change.

Assess- Reassess- Recalibrate

Action

Sit down right now and write your answers to those three questions I just mentioned:

- ✓ What was positive about my day?
- ✓ What was interesting about my day?
- ✓ What was negative about my day?

Once you have completed that, choose one action that can pull one of those negative things up to the positive category. For instance, suppose you said that you did not receive any calls or emails about job proposals you had sent out. You could:

- Call and follow up.
- Send an email.

- Send out more proposals.
- Reassess your proposals.
- Check to see if your proposed prices are within market limits.
- Be creative and give it the time it takes to choose just one action you can do tomorrow.

12
Final Thoughts

If you followed my directives in this book, you should already see results, and your level of procrastination should be reduced. If you are not seeing results- go back to the beginning and DO NOT skip the action items. Do them.

I will make a confession. I kept this book short and to the point for a very specific reason - It was written with you in mind. I could not expect a procrastinator, like myself, to read *War and Peace*. It is meant to be read and reread several times to remind of you of the areas you need to work on to combat procrastination.

In my final thoughts, I wanted to pull out some important points for you to consider and think about as you close this book.

Don't confuse prudence with procrastination. Prudence is using wisdom when looking ahead. Moving at the right time. Faith isn't just moving. Faith is moving when you believe you're being Divinely led to move. Whether you are writing a book, starting a business, moving from being a part time to full time business owner, procrastination occurs when you are only tuned into the voice of the oppressor. Be cautious when you need to be, but move when opportunity is knocking.

Having a clear vision, mission, and values as mentioned in chapter two will help. Remember your Why, because it is what will move and motivate you.

Recognize the voice of the oppressor which manifests itself in fear as discussed in Chapter 3 and perfectionism in Chapter 4. Sometimes it comes in the guise of the fraud police. The inner oppressor's favorite phrase begins "You are not…" and ends with "…enough." Recognize it and delete it from your mind.

Embracing each level of the procrastination prevention pyramid will help you to move based on the Divine voice that's always speaking about the life within you and drown out the voice of the oppressor.

Being able to hear and move to the Divine voice will enable you to acquire the Discipline of Now- learn to clear the channel.

Once you have removed procrastination from your life, you will find your life has been freed up. The next best question is- What are you going to do with all that extra time?

For more information about other programs I have to offer, or if you would just like to give me your perspectives on this book please use the contact information below.

Office: 1-888-812-4705
E-mail: Eric@ericmtwiggs.com
Website: www.ericmtwiggs.com